ME⁻

Transitioning into Young Woman is a Marvelous Journey

Asiyah Davis

lifechronicilespublishing.com
Life Chronicles Publishing
ISBN-13: 978-1-7328944-3-3
Cover Design: Asiyah Davis
Cover Layout
Life Chronicles Publishing
Copyright © 2018

Dedication

I want to dedicate this book to my little sisters Zarah and Meccah-Rose, remember you are loved. Never change who you are to fit in because you are the beam of light that should always shine.

Asiyah

Contents

Poems

1.	You Beam	2
2.	Imagination	4
3.	9-year-old self	6
4.	Your Hair is Magical	8
5.	Young Black Queen	10
6.	11-Year-Old Self	12
7.	You are Connected to the Universe	14
8.	New Beginnings	16
9.	Transition to Middle School	18
10.	12-Year-Old Self	20
11.	Change	22
12.	13	24
13.	Teenage Angst	26
14.	The Girl with A Dream	28
15.	What Do You See?	30
16.	Love is Limitless	32
17.	You are Beauty	36
18.	To the Girl that Cries	38
19.	Leave your mark	42
20.	Forgiveness	44
21.	Always Smile	46
22.	Be You	48

METAMORPH**ISIS**

Metamorph- Change
ISIS- Goddess

You Beam

The universe is within you
With each speckle of dust and bright star
You beam
Because the light within you goes beyond realms
You are a star
Never dim your light

Imagination

Laughter and love
The life of a child
Such freedom and happiness
When your imagination takes you beyond the
physical world and proves the only barriers you have
are the ones you create .
Nurture that inner child
So you can embrace the freedom that coexists with
letting your imagination run wild

9-Year-Old Self

My curls coil in magical ways ,
But why don't they curl like hers ,
Why isn't my hair long and straight?
They say my hair is pretty
But why don't I believe It
I want my hair like hers
Because she gets the attention
I want that attention

Your Hair is Magical

Your hair is beautiful ,
It curls like curly fries, and shines with the sun rise
It sparkles in the light
And defies gravity
The waves created are like the ocean
Subtitle yet beautiful
Everyone wants your curls
Wants to touch the puff
Because it's soft as a pillow
Wants to touch your braids
Because the details
Fold and weave like a quilt
Your hair tells a story that goes beyond generations
They want your hair
Embrace It
Love It
Wear It proudly
Your hair is uniquely formed and crafted
The magic It has within gives you the strength to be
bold
And uniquely you
So be you
They want to be like you
Don't forget that

Young Black Queen

Young black queen
Some may try to take your crown
Or break you down
Take your sense of beauty
And make you feel inadequate
They'll try to make the perception of you
A general impression of you
Negative
Strong
Proud
Loud

All small pieces that coexist within to make you who
you are
They're some of the reasons you shine like a star
And for those of you that are shy
Always hold your head high
Don't disappear cause
It's clear that you're a queen too
To all the young black queens
You are uniquely you
Beautiful
Capable
Smart
And
Powerful too
Your melanin has speckles of the universe flowing
through

And like the moon the sun aluminates your being
Making you the most beautiful thing that steps in a
room
Whatever shade, shape, length and width you are
You truly are the epitome of beauty
So never let anyone take that from you
And if you cry wipe your eyes
And place that crown back on your head
Only you can control your reality
And remember The world is in your hands
So don't forget to shine your light through adversity
because the pain is what truly makes you

A
Young
Black
Queen

11-Year-Old Self

I used to be a young girl
Care free
And happy
Yup that was me
But one day things got complicated
When a red dot appeared on my shorts
My childhood was suddenly confiscated
What was this?
Where did it come from?
Luckily I had my mom to call on
I found out I was no longer a young girl
But now a young lady
A woman in the making
This world was mine for the taking
But then I thought
Could everything still be the same?
Or was maturity suddenly calling my name?
Could I still play with the boys ?
Still be a little girl ?
What did this mean for me ?

That tedious red dot
I thought It was the death of me
But in reality it was the true beginning of my journey
and my destiny
I used to be a young girl
Carefree
And happy
Yup that was me

But now I'm a young woman fulfilling my destiny

You Are Connected to the Universe

The stigma behind It
is all a fluke you see
This thing that happens to you has a purpose and It
flows through you majestically
Like the moon
The stars
And the blue sky
The birds that sing the waves that flow
And the trees that grow and grow
You are one with nature
And nature is one with you

That's the beauty of it all
The interconnectedness we share
The healing
And the children we can bare
You see this is a ever flowing power that flows
Through our veins
And
When we bare pain
We say this name in vein
But what our bodies inhabit during this time
Is simply sublime
You see
Your period is sacred
And This sacredness over turns the pain
All It takes is 3-7 days
And like a flower You'll bloom
Because this sacred time

Nourishes your body
Like the soil nourishes the flower
And as you continue to bloom
Your light within will be able to shine though
Cause this time is sacred
No stigma involved
Embrace it don't deny
But celebrate It
And watch your world evolve

New Beginnings

So unknown and colorful
Like the sun rise
And as you realign your reality
With what's next
You make your sun shine
So never be afraid of a new beginning
Embrace the scarcity of the unknown
Hold the hand of its possibilities
And smile at the multitude of outcomes that
You can and can't control
Cause ultimately
This is your world
And like a new phase
And a new chapter
You have the power to turn your fear
Into love and laughter

Transitioning Into Middle School

As I step up the stairs into the abyss
I'm pondering on questions like what is this?

I'm no longer the top gun in school
I'm new and fresh
But I'm still cool
No more multiple recesses
And time out to play
I'm a big girl now
But does that mean I should change ?
As I take the next step
I walk it with It pride
No more hesitation
A young queen has arrived

12-Year-Old Self

I'm changing
Evolving
In multiple ways
I'm still a girl
But not really the same
I'm taller
leaner
And Maybe a little bit meaner
No longer flat chested
My buds have bloomed
I know I'm sublime
But is this impending doom?

I mean what once was soft skin has
Bumps on It too
I'm starting to feel like a crunch bar
Bumpy but sweet
And there's a cute boy
But what does that really mean?
Exploration of new things
Has me utterly confused
I love my friends
But I think I'm starting to hate school
I wonder about my body
Why doesn't It look like hers?
Something must not be right
And what are all these emotions
Coming at me left and right
One day I'm happy
The next I'm ready to fight

And they got us in class
Learning about our bodies?
This ain't right
I guess this is what happens as you get older
But I'm not ready
And what I want is this to be over
Choo choo all aboard
puberty has arrived and
As I'm forced on this train
I'm just praying I survive

Change

Change is inevitable
It comes all the time
Sometimes you're ready
And others you go in blind
Your body is a temple
And It changes that's simple
One day you have clear skin the next
There's a pimple
But never forget your appearance isn't
All you possess
And when you smile
Yeah that's when you're at your best
I know it's hard
You're not a little girl anymore
More problems are arising
And you're very unsure
But this is a spectacular time
For you, you see
This change is good
And it's meant to be
Just embrace the changes
It'll all be fine
You're beautifully you
You should tell yourself this all the time

No longer a little girl but a young woman
Your quilt has been started
And this chapter has already been woven
So smile relax
This is truly meant to be

Just remember change is inevitable
And It comes naturally

13

When I look into the mirror
I see limitless potential
I see a queen
who is very influential
I'm smart
athletic
Loving and kind
And my imagination runs wild
Giving me a powerful mind
Care free
And young it's one in the same
But responsibility beckons
This is no longer a game
I'm still finding myself and
Exploring what's next
I've evolved but I'm the same
As my age continues to progress
When I look in the mirror
All I see is me
But Not the same 12 year old
Cause now I'm thirteen

Teenage Angst

When you become A teen
Everything is a blur
There's boys
Girls
And angst everywhere
As you continue to grow there's a lot you don't know
You'll learn through lessons
And your emotions may show
But you're a strong girl
And everything works in your favor
Whether bad or good in time
Every lesson will make you better
Thirteen is the start of a new chapter
You're still a young girl
But a young adult comes shortly after
Enjoy the time you have as a kid
Because time moves fast
Love yourself and put everything else last
The drama the boys
The girls are irrelevant
You're a beautiful girl
And you're truly magnificent
Once you become a teen you think you want to be
grown
But don't rush It enjoy your teens
It's not always fun being on your own .
Love yourself
And Enjoy this time
Welcome to your teen
Make sure you enjoy the ride

The Girl With A Dream

To the girl with a dream
Your dream is valid
Attainable
And true
Don't let anyone take it away from you
It's not far-fetched
Un realistic
Or crazy
If you can imagine It
You can see It
And if you see It
You should believe It
It doesn't matter how others perceive It
Your dreams are beautiful thoughts
And those thoughts can come alive
All you need is a little faith and a lot of drive
This universe has no boundaries
And this is your world to run
So go after that dream
And have a little fun
Cause if you do what you love
You'll love what you do
No matter how young or old you are
You're a star
Don't; let negative thoughts take that away from you
Young girl with a dream
Dream big
Cause it'll all come true
If nobody does

You should always believe in you!

What Do You See?

When you look in the mirror what do you see ?
Look deep past your looks
And all in between
If you're beautiful in the inside
It will radiate through
So nourish your soul
So It can truly nourish you
Be kind and sweet
And never deceitful
Move with love
And love will move through you
And break any form of evil
Be empathetic and thoughtful
And love all your peers
Especially the ones that
Need help and are full of fears
If you help one another
You can never be stopped
The world is yours for the taking
And there's nowhere to go
But the top
So act with good intentions
And be true to you
Love yourself
so your light will
Be able to Shine through
No matter what shape, shade, or size you are
What's in the mirror
Is just an appearance
And what's inside is who you really are

So Love both
What's inside and out
Cause they make you, you
And If you're true
Then no hateful words or thoughts
Should be able to break you
when you look in the mirror what do you see ?
You should see
A beautiful reflection
And a light that shines majestically

Love is Limitless

Love has no boundaries
No limits
No hate
Or shame
It's a beautiful word that shouldn't be used in vein
Love is not just a feeling
It's a frequency that
Hits you like the waves hitting the shore
Full force and transparent
And although it's scary It can have you begging for
more
Just like the waves hit the shore
You get It?
A wave doesn't just describe water
Frequencies have waves too
And love is just a word
But all are interconnected
And flow with ease around the world
So why do we love?
It's such an anomaly
Love is beautiful and pure
And It can reach everybody
There's self-love
And loving others no matter who they are
Love is not judgement it's acceptance even when we
question who we are
If you love what makes you uncomfortable
Even if It regards someone else
you can reconstruct any perception and construct
that has been created to bring division because love

has the power to win above anything else
Hate is a word that is delectable and hard to debate
We hate when we love
we love when we hate
Both can be a result of the other
But try your best not to hate one another
You see they want us to hate
Cause if we love
There's no power to control with no debate
Love is the highest frequency try to always move in
love
Even when hate arises
And anger is true
What's in your power is how you take It
and make It relatable to you
It takes just as much energy to hate
As to love
Not saying that with love
Hurt feelings aren't involved
But it's better to love than to hate
Cause when you hate bad energy is involved
And bad energy will dim your light
So choose love
Cause It will brighten all darkness
And others will follow
Without Love people will wallow
Your smile
Your tone
Your energy let alone
Has the power to spread your love
Don't put anything else above

Without knowing your presence can affect one
another
While moving In love you
Can protect one another
So chose It
Don't fight It
Be love and ignite It

You are Beauty

By definition beauty is
the quality or qualities in a person or thing that gives
pleasure to the senses or pleasurably exalts the mind
or spirit
But beauty has no words that bind It to be true
Beauty is a thought that leads to an expression
It's a construct in the mind
Purely based off of perception
Beauty is the leaves that drift from the trees and hit
the ground when fall comes along

It's the intricate details that form to shape the
spectacle Of a snowflake
It's the multitude of blues and whites that bind
together in the waves that calmly move back and
forth creating peace
It's the flowers that bloom
It's me
And it's you
We're all interconnected
And if you find yourself liking Someone that doesn't
see your beauty
Don't be sad
Cause if they see the beauty in the world they see
the beauty in you .
Cause we are all interconnected
Formed and created
Beautifully ourselves
And if one doesn't appreciate It
You have to believe it yourself

Acceptance of one's own beauty puts you above the
rest
You're truly beautiful
Any one can attest
Don't ever be down or let
Yourself feel in lack when it comes to beauty
If there's one thing
You can control it's the way you view yourself
You're beautifully you don't
Put that beauty on a shelf

To the Girl that Cries

To the girl that Cries
It's okay
Not in a sense to where whatever happened is okay
but
It's okay
You'll get through It
You're amazing
There's nothing to It
People love you even when you feel they don't
Some people are given tough realities
There's no particular person who won't
I can't say don't cry
Or wipe your eyes and be strong
Because honestly it's okay to cry and be vulnerable
so that you can move along
Life is like a road forever winding and bending in
places you least expect . But like a car you can
control the way you react and weave on that road to
whatever is next
Like I said you are loved even when you feel alone
Whatever problem you have now may not even be a
problem down the road
Your mind is a powerful thing
You can control what truly affects you
And for the girl that's truly hurting I'm sorry for your
pain that has vexed you
No words can explain or take away how you feel
Try to laugh, and smile
positivity and love will help lighten that weight for a
while

You see whether you want to believe It or not
your pain has a purpose
It's here to mold
And Shape you
Here to Push you to be the best individual you can be
Here to allow you to connect with those who harbor
that same pain
Here to show you that you're resilient and able to
prevail and outlast the pain that calls your name
To the girl that cries don't wipe your eyes keep
crying and address how you feel
But just know there's a light within you that will
shine through enveloping all darkness that surrounds
you
You're unique
Beautiful
Strong
And truly inspirational
Unequivocally you
Which makes you motivational
To that girl that cries because she's hurting
Like frozen let It go
Good things are coming

Write your own poem.

Leave Your Mark

As you stand on the hill
You feel the wet grass between your toes
The cold breeze bringing the fresh scent of flowers
up to your nose
Look upon the horizon and relish at the world
The clouds the sky
The birds that fly by
The bees buzzing around
The animals running
making a faint sound
This is nature
This is the world
The simplicity of actions that are taken in front of
you
Is what makes It all so beautiful
What makes you beautiful
After all you are one with nature
So connect
Put the phone down
Put the tablet down
Leave the screens and run wild
Run free
Roll in the grass or hug a tree
Feel the energy of the world around you
You are a part of this world
Just one girl
With a big task
Leaving your mark
To help make this earth last

Forgiveness

To forgive is to let go
To let go is to move on
To move on is to create a memory not a present
experience
Remember hurt people
Hurt people
So try not to allow someone to hurt you
But if you do
Don't forget to forgive
Because when you forgive you allow yourself to live
To love
To move past the pain
And rise above
Forgiveness is setting yourself free
But before you can forgive someone else never
forget to forgive yourself

Always Smile

Smile even when It hurts
Smile when you're at your worst
Smile when you have it all
Smile when you're about to fall
Smile when you pass a test
Smile when you're at your best
Smile walking down the hall
Smile when you've lost It all
The moral of the story is to smile
All the time
And if you never smile
Then you're wasting all your time
But if you try to smile
Every chance you get
You'll show the world your spark
And you'll never throw a fit

Be You

As you continue to embark on this transition
Never let a thought sway you from your position
Strong
Resilient
Powerful
That's you
You're beautiful inside and out
Don't let anything or anyone take that away from
you
Always remember you have support and you are
loved
Don't push the help away
embrace it with a hug
Know that it's okay to seek advice
and take what's relatable to you
This is only a time of growth
Don't let any darkness envelope you
Search for what you love
and love what you do this is your time to shine
So, try to enjoy this time
Always try to spread the frequency of love
and love will come back to you
And most importantly don't forget to smile
It will make this time worth while
It's time to say goodbye to being a baby
and welcome this beautiful transition
into becoming
YOUNG
LADY

Hello beautiful young ladies,

These series of poems were created based out of my experiences as a young lady and how I felt not only in my own skin but emotionally and mentally as well. Puberty, transitioning and going to school can be kind of hard at times, some of your peers may be rude, some may be shy, some may want to embarrass you, and some may want to be your friend. But what's most important is how you hold yourself accountable for being authentically you, and not letting anyone, whether a friend or foe make you want to be someone else.

You are AMAZING, BEAUTIFUL, SMART, STRONG, UNIQUE, and so much more. I know it may get rough and you may feel alone. Remember first, almost every other girl your age is going through the same thing, and also if you have a sister, an aunt, mom, grandma, or any influential guardian of some sort that is a woman in your life they've been through what you're going through. So never feel ashamed to ask for help or advice.

This transition is like a metamorphosis, as a kid, you're a pretty fuzzy caterpillar, and during this transition, you start shielding yourself in a cocoon protecting who you, and who you're becoming. But when you come to the end of this transition the cocoon breaks, and you come out a beautiful butterfly ready to fly and show the world your colorful complex yet beautiful wings.

So never forget you are a staggeringly beautiful butterfly with limitless potential and as you fly around don't forget to leave a beautiful positive mark on those around you.

This is not only a transition this is your METAMORPHOSIS!

Write your own poems.

Write your own poems.

Made in the USA
Middletown, DE
06 March 2019